CONSTITUTION ON THE SACRED LITURGY

(Sacrosanctum Concilium)

Introduction by
Francis Cardinal Arinze
Emeritus Prefect, Congregation for Divine Worship
and the Discipline of the Sacraments

VATICAN COUNCIL II

CATHOLIC TRUTH SOCIETY
PUBLISHERS TO THE HOLY SEE

Contents

INTRODUCTION
by Francis Cardinal Arinze

The celebration of the mysteries of our redemption, especially of the paschal mystery of the suffering, death and resurrection of Our Lord and Saviour Jesus Christ in the Sacred Liturgy, is central in and to the life of the Church. Participation in liturgical celebrations is seen by the Second Vatican Council as the primary and indispensable source "from which the faithful may be expected to draw the true Christian spirit" (SC, no. 14).

It was, therefore, very fitting that the first of the sixteen documents to be issued by the Second Vatican Council was on the Sacred Liturgy. As *Sacrosanctum Concilium* was promulgated on December 4 1963, "the first fruit of the Council" (VQA, no. 1) was offered to the entire Church. Through the rich doctrine and wise directives offered by this Constitution, the road to liturgical renewal was marked out for the Church "in accordance with the conciliar principles of fidelity to tradition and openness to legitimate development" (VQA, no. 4; cf also SC, no. 23).

The crucial role of *Sacrosanctum Concilium* becomes clearer when we consider that a very close and organic bond does exist between sound liturgical renewal and the renewal of the whole life of the Church. After all, "the liturgy is the peak towards which the Church's activity tends, just as it is also the fountain-head from which all its vitality flows" (SC, no. 10). "The Church not only acts but also expresses herself in the liturgy and draws from the liturgy the strength for her life" (DC, no. 13). In particular, "the Church draws her life from the Eucharist" (EE, no. 1), "the fount and apex of the whole Christian life" (LG, no. 11).

In the liturgical life of the Church, some very good developments have taken place since *Sacrosanctum Concilium* was promulgated. Pope John Paul II, in commemoration of twenty-five years of the document, lists five of these positive results (VQA no. 12).

The first is the place given to the Bible in the liturgy. *Sacrosanctum Concilium* insisted that the table of God's word is to be made more abundantly available to the people of God in the liturgy. If we reflect back over the past forty years, we see how the renewed liturgical rites have been made much richer with biblical texts. In the Mass, the lectionary is so arranged as to cover most of the Bible in a three-year Sunday reading and a two-year weekday lessons programme. The responsorial psalms help to elucidate the readings. The sacramental rites and the celebrations of the sacramentals are suitably fitted with rich biblical texts. So is the Liturgy of the Hours. In this way not only are the faithful exposed, as it were, to a greater part of Holy Scripture so as to become more familiar with it, but each community has the opportunity, in the specific setting of the liturgical celebration, to enter ever more deeply at all the levels of the human person into the great mystery of God's transforming love which the Scripture proclaims. In country after country, immense effort is undertaken to provide the Christian people with translations of the Bible.

A second happy development is the sustained effort to translate the various liturgical texts into the current language of the people, and also to face the challenges of adapting liturgical celebration to the culture of each people.

A third reason for gratitude is "the increased participation of the faithful by prayer and song, gesture and silence, in the Eucharist and the other sacraments".

We are also encouraged because of "the ministries exercised by lay people and the responsibilities that they have assumed in virtue of the common priesthood into which they have been initiated through Baptism and Confirmation".

Lastly, and as a summary of the above four areas, we must thank God "for the radiant vitality of so many Christian communities, a vitality drawn from the wellspring of the liturgy".

Each of these five positive results offers us reasons for joy and encouragement. But each also assigns us a further task, poses us a challenge and enjoins on us to see that the developments remain truly positive, according to the desire and directives of the Council expressed in *Sacrosanctum Concilium*, and of the Pope and the Bishops who guide us today and tomorrow in the Church that Christ founded.

Bible and Liturgy

In his commentary on Isaiah, St Jerome tells us that, "Ignorance of the Scriptures is ignorance of Christ". Ignorance of the Bible is a great handicap to an understanding of the liturgy and the hoped-for fruit of participation in its celebration. A great part of the liturgy is based on Holy Scripture, not only in the readings but also in the inspiration of the prayers, in the symbols and in the images dear to the public worship of the Church. Without a biblical understanding of exodus, covenant, chosen people, Isaac, paschal lamb, Passover, manna and promised land, how can the liturgy be understood? The Psalms, in particular, are an indispensable source of liturgical language, signs and prayers.

"The Church is nourished on the word of God as written down in the books of the Old and New Testaments. When the Church proclaims the word in the liturgy, she welcomes it as a way in which Christ is present" (VL, no. 23). It is Christ "himself who speaks when the Holy Scriptures are read in the Church" (SC, no. 7).

Everyone in the Church needs to make progress in contact with the Bible: clerics, consecrated people and the lay faithful. The growing desire of many lay people to receive better and deeper biblical formation should be met with adequate programmes. The translation of the Bible into the people's language is the first and indispensable step. People also need guidance individually and in groups in how to read, understand and pray the Bible. This is essential for a Catholic approach to the Bible, in which it is clearly understood that it is the Church which presents the Bible to the faithful, explaining its significance in the light of the Tradition that goes back to the Lord's Apostles. Liturgical experts and pastors should help people to see how selected biblical texts fit into specific liturgical celebrations. Homilies should also be rich in biblical foundations.

Translation - Adaptation - Inculturation

The Second Vatican Council introduced the vernacular into the liturgy and also allowed for properly considered adaptations and inculturation in the rites. This poses a considerable challenge and requires careful consideration.

While retaining Latin as the language in the Latin rite, the Council appreciated the usefulness of the use of the mother tongue among the various peoples of the world (cf. SC, no. 36). However, Vatican II did not abolish Latin. It would be good that occasionally a parish sings the more popular parts of the Mass in Latin: think of what this means in terms of preserving and respecting our patrimony, showing the Church as a community that has a memory, and facilitating international Eucharistic celebrations.

Liturgical translations into the mother tongue pose the demanding challenge of producing translations which are faithful to the Latin original, which are excellent literary productions, which can be set to music, which will stand the test of time and which will nourish the piety and spiritual sensitivity of the people. Dangers and abuses arise from *ex tempore* translations, hurried works and illegitimate translations not approved by the Conference of Bishops and ratified by the Apostolic See.

When we go into the area of adaptation and inculturation of rites, we are faced with still more demanding challenges. *Sacrosanctum Concilium* is very clear in its principles and directives (SC, no. 37). The carrying out of these directives will engage the Church for generations, especially in the countries of recent evangelization. Writing on the Holy Eucharist, Pope John Paul II says that "the 'treasure' is too important and precious to risk impoverishment or compromise through forms of experimentation or practices introduced without a careful review on the part of the competent ecclesiastical authorities ... 'because the Sacred Liturgy expresses and celebrates the faith professed by all, and being the heritage of the whole Church, cannot be determined by local Churches in isolation from the universal Church'" (EE, no. 51).

It is therefore reasonable and indeed obvious that there must be liturgical regulations and norms. With reference to the Holy Eucharist, for example, Pope John Paul II says that "These norms are a concrete expression of the authentically ecclesial nature of the Eucharist; this is their deepest meaning. Liturgy is never anyone's private properly, be it of the celebrant or of the community" (EE, no. 52). That is why *Sacrosanctum Concilium* already declared that the regulation of the sacred liturgy depends solely on the authority of the Church, that is, on the Apostolic See and, as laws may determine, on the Bishops and the Bishops' Conference. "Wherefore, no one else at all, not even a priest, may, of his own authority, add to, take from, or modify anything in the Liturgy" (SC, no. 22).

The danger is that some people seem to think that inculturation in the liturgy encourages free and uncontrolled creativity. Pope John Paul writes that "it must be lamented that, especially in the years following the post-conciliar liturgical reform, as a result of a misguided sense of creativity and adaptation, there have been a number of *abuses* which have been a source of suffering for many" (EE, no. 52).

True and lasting inculturation demands long study, discussions among experts in interdisciplinary platforms, examination and decision by Bishops, recognition from the Apostolic See and prudent presentation to the people of God. Moreover, it should be noted that in religious matters, people's sensitivity and piety can easily be hurt by ill-considered and hasty novelties. In religious practices, most people are understandably conservative in the good sense, and unwilling to endure frequent changes.

Active Participation

The Fathers of the Second Vatican Council stress the importance of the active participation of all the faithful in liturgical celebrations. "Mother Church greatly desires that all the faithful may be brought to take that full, intelligent, active part in liturgical celebrations which the nature of the Liturgy itself requires, and which, in virtue of their baptism, is the right and duty of the Christian people, 'a chosen race, a royal priesthood, a holy nation, God's own people' (*1 Pet* 2:9; cf. 2:4-5)" (SC, no. 14).

It is important to realize that the internal aspect of participation is indispensable as a basis, a requirement and the aim of all external participation. That is why personal prayer, Scriptural meditation and moments of silence are necessary. "The sacred Liturgy is not the whole of the Church's activity. Before men can come to the Liturgy, they must be called to faith and to conversion" (SC, no. 9). It is highly advisable to promote moments of silence for individual reflection and prayer during the Eucharistic celebration, at such times as after each reading, and after the homily and Holy Communion. Choirs should resist the temptation to fill every available quiet time with singing.

A sense of reverence and devotion is conducive to interiorized active participation. Prominent among those who influence the congregation in this matter is the priest celebrant. But the altar servers, the readers, the choir and the extraordinary ministers of Holy Communion where they are really needed, do also influence the people by every move of theirs. Reverence is the exterior manifestation of faith. It should show our sense of adoration of God most holy and most high. And our belief in the Real Presence of Jesus Christ in the Holy Eucharist should come across in how the ministers handle the Blessed Sacrament, how they genuflect and how they recite the prescribed prayers.

Liturgical music promotes worship. The Gregorian chant has an honoured place in the history of the Latin rite. It is to be noted that even young people today do appreciate it. Most liturgical singing will understandably be in the mother tongue. The Diocesan or National Music Commission should see that such texts are suitable from the theological and musical points of view before they are approved for Church use.

The *General Instruction on the Roman Missal* wisely notes the importance of common gestures by the worshipping congregation (nos. 42-44). Examples are times for the congregation to stand, kneel or sit. Bishops' Conferences can and do make some specifications. Care should be taken not to regiment the congregation, as if it were an army. Some flexibility should be allowed, more so as it is easy to hurt people's eucharistic sensitivity - with reference, for example, to kneeling or standing.

Church architecture also influences active participation. If a

8

church is built and the seats are arranged as in an amphitheatre or as in a banquet, the undeclared emphasis may be horizontal attention to one another, rather than vertical attention to God. In this sense the celebration of Mass facing the people demands from the priest and altar servers a high level of discipline, so that as from the offertory of the Mass it be seen clearly that both priest and people are turned towards God, not towards one another. We come to Mass primarily to adore God, not to affirm one another, although this is not excluded.

Some people think that liturgical renewal means the removal of kneelers from Church pews, the knocking down of altar rails or the positioning of the altar in the middle of the sitting area of the people. The Church has never said any such thing. Nor does liturgical restoration mean iconoclasm or the removal of all statues and sacred images. These should be displayed, albeit with good judgment. And the altar of the Blessed Sacrament should be outstanding for its beauty and honored prominence, otherwise in some so-called restored churches one could rightly lament: "They have taken my Lord away, and I don't know where they have put him" (*Jn* 20:13).

Lay Liturgical Roles

For proper celebration of the sacred liturgy and fruitful participation in it by all Christ's faithful, it is important to understand the roles proper to the ministerial or ordained priest and those proper to the lay faithful. Christ is the priest, the high priest. He gives all baptized people a share in this role of offering gifts to God. The common priesthood of all the baptized gives people the capacity to offer Christian worship, to offer Christ to the Eternal Father through the hands of the ordained priest at the Eucharistic celebration, to receive the sacraments and to live holy lives and by self-denial and active charity make of their entire lives a sacrifice.

The ministerial priest, on the other hand, is a man chosen from among the baptized and ordained by the Bishop to the Sacrament of Holy Orders. He alone can consecrate bread into the Body of Christ

9

and wine into the Blood of Christ and offer to the Eternal Father in the name of Christ and the whole Christian people. It is clear that, though they differ from one another in essence and not only in degree, the common priesthood of all the baptized and the ministerial or hierarchical priesthood are closely related (cf. LG, no. 10).

The major challenge is to help the lay faithful appreciate their dignity as baptized persons. From this follows their role at the Eucharistic sacrifice and other liturgical acts. They are the people of God. They are insiders. Their share as readers of lessons, as leaders of song and as the people offering with and through the priest is based on Baptism. The high point is when they communicate at the Eucharistic table. This crowns their participation at the Eucharistic sacrifice.

There should be no attempt to clericalize the laity. This could happen when, for example, lay people chosen as extraordinary ministers of Holy Communion no longer see this role as being called on to help when the ordinary ministers (bishop, priest and deacon) are not available in sufficient numbers to cope with the high number of communicants.

We have also the opposite mistake of trying to laicize the clergy. When the priest no longer wishes to bless the people with the formula "May Almighty God bless you", but prefers the seemingly democratic wording, "May Almighty God bless us", then we have a confusion of roles. The same thing happens when some priests think that they should not concelebrate a Mass but should just participate as lay people in order to show more solidarity with the lay faithful. "In liturgical celebrations, each participant, whether minister or simple member of the faithful, in the performance of his office, is to do all that and only that which belongs to him from the nature of things and the rules of liturgy" (SC, no. 28).

Conclusion: Revitalization of Church Life

There is no doubt that *Sacrosanctum Concilium* has continued to sustain the Church along the paths of holiness by fostering genuine liturgical life. It remains important to see that the Council's genuine directives are actually followed.

Introduction

It is a fact that as the Pope says, "some have received the new books with a certain indifference, or without trying to understand the reasons for the changes; others, unfortunately, have turned back in a one-sided and exclusive way to the previous liturgical forms which some of them consider to be the sole guarantee of certainty in the faith" (VQA, no. 11). Ongoing formation continues to be necessary.

Moreover we have to note that the liturgy of the Church goes beyond the liturgical reform. Many young priests, consecrated brothers and sisters and lay faithful are not conversant with the liturgical books of fifty years ago, either because they were born after Vatican II, or because they were infants when it was celebrated. What is above all needed is "an ever deeper grasp of the liturgy of the Church, celebrated according to the current books and lived above all as a reality in the spiritual order" (VQA, no. 14). There should be a widespread formation of the lay faithful in the theology and spirituality of the liturgy.

✠ **Francis Cardinal Arinze**
*Emeritus Prefect, Congregation for Divine Worship
and the Discipline of the Sacraments*

Abbreviations
DC - Dominicae Cenae
EE - Ecclesia de Eucharistia
LG - Lumen Gentium
SC - Sacrosanctum Concilium
VQA - Vicesimus Quintus Annus
VL - Varietates Legitimae

11

PAUL, BISHOP
SERVANT OF THE SERVANTS OF GOD
TOGETHER WITH THE FATHERS
OF THE SACRED COUNCIL PUTS ON
PERMANENT RECORD THE

CONSTITUTION
ON THE SACRED LITURGY

1. THE SACRED COUNCIL has set itself the following aims: to increase daily among the faithful the vigour of their Christian life; to adapt in the best way possible to the needs of our time those institutions that admit of change; to foster anything at all that may contribute to the union of all those who believe in Christ; to give added support to anything that may help to call all men into the bosom of the Church. For the better achievement of these aims, it considers that it should give particular attention to the restoration and encouragement of the Liturgy.

2. The reason for this is that the Liturgy, by which is put into effect, especially in the divine sacrifice of the Eucharist, 'the work of our redemption',[1] contributes in the highest measure to enabling the faithful to express in their lives and show forth to others the mystery of Christ and the real nature of the true Church. It is, of course, characteristic of the Church to be at once human and divine, visible and yet endowed with invisible values, pulsating with activity and yet given over to contemplation, present in the world and withal a stranger there. In all this there is order: the human in the Church is ordered to and, indeed, subordinate to the divine, the visible to the invisible, action to contemplation, the present to the city which is to

---

[1] *Roman Missal*, Ninth Sunday after Pentecost, Prayer over the Offerings.

come, that we seek.[2] With the result that, whereas the Liturgy daily builds up those who are in the Church into a holy temple in the Lord, into a dwelling place of God in the Spirit,[3] until they attain to the measure of the stature of the fullness of Christ,[4] it gives them, at the same time, a remarkably increased vitality for the publishing abroad of Christ, and, by so doing, to those who are outside her confines, displays the Church as an ensign raised up for the nations,[5] an ensign under which may be gathered into one the children of God who are scattered abroad,[6] until there be but one flock and one shepherd.[7]

3. Therefore, the Sacred Council thinks it advisable, firstly, to restate the following principles which apply in the matter of encouraging and restoring the Liturgy, and, secondly, to fix certain practical guiding lines.

Among these principles and guiding lines, there are some that can and ought to be applied both to the Roman rite and to all the other rites, but it must be clearly understood that the practical directions that follow concern the Roman rite only, except when they treat of matters which, from the very nature of things, affect the other rites also.

4. Finally, remaining in this matter faithful to tradition, the Sacred Council declares that Holy Mother Church holds all legitimately recognized rites in equal right and honour, and that she wishes them to be kept and fostered unreservedly for the future. The Council desires that, where there may be need, they should be carefully and thoroughly revised in accordance with sound tradition and endowed with a new vigour to suit the needs and circumstances of the present day.

---

[2] Cf. *Heb* 13:14.
[3] Cf. *Eph* 2:21-2.
[4] Cf. *Eph* 4:13.
[5] Cf. *Js* 11:12.
[6] Cf. *Jn* 11:52.
[7] Cf. *Jn* 10:16.

CHAPTER I

GENERAL PRINCIPLES GOVERNING THE RESTORATION AND ENCOURAGEMENT OF THE SACRED LITURGY

I. THE NATURE OF THE SACRED LITURGY AND ITS IMPORTANCE IN THE LIFE OF THE CHURCH

5. God, 'who desires all men to be saved and to come to the knowledge of the truth' (1 *Tim* 2:4), 'in many and various ways spoke of old to our fathers by the prophets' (*Heb* 1:1) and, when the fullness of time had come, sent his Son, the Word made flesh, anointed by the Holy Spirit, to preach good news to the poor, to bind up the brokenhearted,[8] 'the one physician at once both flesh and spirit',[9] the mediator between God and man.[10] His humanity, in the Word's oneness of Person, was the instrument by which our salvation was effected, and that is why we can say that in Christ 'the perfect satisfaction required for our reconciliation has been already made, and on us has been bestowed the whole fullness of divine worship'.[11]

This work - the redemption of mankind and the perfect glorification of God - was foretold by the mighty works of God wrought on behalf of the people of the Old Testament and effectively accomplished by the Lord Christ, above all in the

---

[8] Cf. *Is* 61:1; *Lk* 4:18.
[9] *St Ignatius of Antioch, Ad Ephesios*, 7,2.
[10] Cf. *1 Tim* 2:5.
[11] *Sacramentarium Veronese (Leonianum)*; Ed. C. MOHLBERG, Rome, 1956, No. 1265, p.162.

paschal mystery of his blessed Passion, his Resurrection from the nether world and his glorious Ascension. In this paschal mystery 'he destroyed death by his dying and remade life by his rising',[12] for, from the side of Christ sleeping on the cross the wondrous sacrament of the whole Church came forth.[13]

6. So then, as Christ was sent by the Father, even so did he send the apostles, filled with the Holy Spirit, to preach the gospel to the whole creation[14] and to proclaim that the Son of God, by his death and resurrection, had rescued us from the power of Satan[15] and from death, and transferred us to the Father's kingdom. At the same time, the work of salvation they were making known, this same work they were to put into effect, through the sacrifice and the sacraments round which, of course, all liturgical life revolves. For, in baptism men are grafted into Christ's paschal mystery - they die with him, they are buried with him, they are raised with him.[16] They receive the Spirit of adoption into sonship 'in which we cry, "Abba! Father!"' (*Rom* 8:15) and so become true worshippers, such as the Father seeks to worship him.[17] Likewise, each time they eat the Lord's Supper, they proclaim his death until he comes.[18] For this reason, on the day of Pentecost, the very day on which the Church appeared before the world, 'those who received [Peter's] word were baptized'. 'And they devoted themselves to the apostles' teaching and fellowship, to the breaking of bread and the prayers ... praising God and having favour with all the people' (*Acts* 2:41-7). From that day on, the Church has never failed to assemble together for the celebration of the paschal mystery, reading 'in all the scriptures the things concerning [Christ]' (*Lk* 24:27), celebrating the Eucharist in

---

[12] *Roman Missal*, Preface for Easter.
[13] Cf. St Augustine, Enarr. in Ps., 138, 2 (*Corpus Christianorum*, 40, Turnhout, 1956, p. 1991); *Roman Missal*, Collect after the second prophecy on Holy Saturday (before the 1956 reform).
[14] Cf. *Mk* 16:15.
[15] Cf. *Acts* 26:18.
[16] Cf. *Rom* 6:4; *Eph* 2:6; *Col* 3:1, 2 *Tim* 2:11.
[17] Cf. *Jn* 4:23.
[18] Cf. *I Cor* 11:26.

which 'are set forth the victory and triumph of his death',[19] and also giving thanks 'to God for his inexpressible gift' (2 *Cor* 9:15) in Christ Jesus, in 'praise of his glory' (*Eph* 1:12) through the power of the Holy Spirit.

7. For the perfect and complete accomplishment of this great work Christ is ever present in his Church, more particularly in her liturgical acts. He is present in the sacrifice of the Mass, first of all in the person of the minister - 'he now offers himself by the ministry of priests, who then offered himself on the cross'[20], - but chiefly under the eucharistic species [of bread and wine]. His presence is realized, by his active power, in the sacraments, for whenever anyone baptizes, it is Christ himself who baptizes.[21] His presence is realized, by his spoken word, since it is he himself who speaks when the Holy Scriptures are read in the Church. Finally, his presence is realized when the Church makes supplication and sings, his presence who promised that 'where two or three are gathered in my name, there am I in the midst of them' (*Mt* 18:20).

It is true to say that Christ always joins with himself in this great work, in which God is perfectly glorified and men sanctified, the Church his most dearly loved Bride: she calls upon her Lord and through him presents her worship to the Eternal Father.

It is, therefore, only right to see in the Liturgy the exercise of Jesus Christ's priestly office. For, in the Liturgy, first, by means of sensible signs the sanctification of man is both signified and, in a manner proper to each sign, brought about; second, by the Mystical Body of Jesus Christ, of the Head, that is to say, and its members, there is carried out a complete public worship.

From this it follows that every liturgical celebration, inasmuch as it is a work of Christ the Priest and of his Body the Church, is

---

[19] COUNCIL OF TRENT, Sess. XIII, Decree *De Ss. Eucharistia*, 5 (DENZ, 878; *Concilium Tridentium*, Ed. Gorres-Gesellschaft, 7, 4, Freiburg, 1961, p. 202).
[20] COUNCIL OF TRENT, Sess. XXII, Doctrine De Ss. *Missae Sacrificio*, 2 (Denz. 940; Ed. Cit., 8,5, p. 960).
[21] St Augustine, *In Ioann. Ev*. Tr., 6, 1, 7; PL 35, 1428.

pre-eminently a sacred action, the efficacy of which no other act of the Church can equal on the same basis and to the same degree.

8. In our liturgy here on earth, we receive a foretaste of and a share in the heavenly liturgy that is celebrated in the holy city Jerusalem towards which we are wending our pilgrim way and in which Christ is, seated at the right hand of God, a minister in the sanctuary and the true tabernacle.[22] With all the host of the army of heaven we join in singing to the Lord the hymn of glory. Reverencing the memory of the saints, we hope for some part and fellowship with them. We await the Saviour our Lord Jesus Christ until the day when he who is our life appears, and we appear with him in glory.[23]

9. The sacred Liturgy is not the whole of the Church's activity. Before men can come to the Liturgy, they must be called to faith and conversion. 'How are men to call upon him in whom they have not believed? And how are they to believe in him of whom they have not heard? And how are they to hear without a preacher? And how can men preach unless they are sent?' (*Rom* 10:14-15).

The Church, therefore, proclaims to unbelievers the message of salvation to the end that all men may come to know the only true God and Jesus Christ whom he has sent, and may repent and turn from their own ways.[24] As for the believers, she must ever preach to them faith and repentance; she must also fit them for the sacraments, teach them to observe all that Christ has commanded,[25] and encourage them in all those works of charity, devotion and apostolate that make it obvious that Christians, though they are not of this world, are yet the light of the world, glorifying the Father in the sight of men.

10. Nevertheless, the Liturgy is the peak towards which the Church's activity tends, just as it is also the fountain-head from

---

[22] Cf. *Rev* 21:2; *Col* 3:1; *Heb* 8:2.
[23] Cf. *Phil* 3:20; *Col* 3:4.
[24] Cf. *Lk* 24:27; *Jn* 17:3; *Acts* 2:38.
[25] Cf. *Mt* 28:20.

which all its vitality flows. For the labours of the apostolate have but one end, namely, that all men made God's sons by faith and baptism should be drawn together, praise God in the midst of the Church, share in the sacrifice and eat the Lord's Supper.

In return, the Liturgy moves the faithful whom it has heaped with the delights of 'the paschal sacraments' to be 'of one mind in the service of God',[26] and prays that 'they may hold fast in their everyday life what they have received in faith'.[27] Furthermore, the renewal of the Lord's covenant with men in the Eucharist attracts the faithful to and fires them with the compelling love of Christ. And so, from the Liturgy, and especially from the Eucharist, grace flows out into us as from a fountain, procuring with the greatest possible effect that sanctification of men in Christ and that glorification of God which are the end of all the other works of the Church.

11. In order that this full effect may be realized, it is, however, essential that the faithful should come to the Liturgy in the right frame of mind, suiting their thoughts to their voices and cooperating with the grace from on high, lest they receive it in vain.[28] Therefore, pastors must see to it, on the one hand, that in the performance of the liturgy the laws of valid and licit celebration are observed, and, on the other hand, that the faithful take part in its performance intelligently, actively and fruitfully.

12. However, the spiritual life is not limited to participation in the sacred Liturgy and nothing but that. For the Christian, called to take part in common prayer, must also go into his private room and pray to the Father in secret,[29] or rather, as the apostle teaches, pray

[26] *Roman Missal*, Easter Sunday, Postcommunion.
[27] *Ibid.* Tuesday in Easter Week, Collect.
[28] Cf. *2 Cor* 6:1.
[29] Cf. *Mt* 6:6.

without ceasing.[30] We are further taught by the same apostle always to carry in our body the death of Jesus, so that the life of Jesus, also, may be manifested in our mortal flesh.[31] For this reason, we pray the Lord in the sacrifice of the Mass that he would accept the offering of our spiritual victim and make for himself of our selves an everlasting offering'.[32]

13. The devotional practices of the Christian people, provided they are in agreement with the Church's laws and directives, are warmly recommended, especially when it is the Apostolic See that has ordered them.

A special dignity is also enjoyed by such pious practices of particular Churches as are performed by order of the bishops in accordance with properly approved customs or books.

However, taking account of the liturgical seasons, these exercises are to be so arranged as to conform with the sacred Liturgy, flow from it, as it were, and lead the people to it, for the Liturgy is, of its nature, far superior to them.

II. TEACHING THE LITURGY
AND ACTIVE PARTICIPATION
IN THE LITURGY

14. Mother Church greatly desires that all the faithful may be brought to take that full, intelligent, active part in liturgical celebrations which the nature of the Liturgy itself requires, and which, in virtue of their baptism, is the right and duty of the Christian people, 'a chosen race, a royal priesthood, a holy nation, God's own people' (1 *Pet* 2:9; cf. 2:4-5).

This full, active participation on the part of the whole people is something that deserves the utmost attention when the reformation and fostering of the sacred Liturgy are under consideration, because

---

[30] *1 Thess* 5:17.
[31] Cf. *2 Cor* 4:10-11.
[32] *Roman Missal*, Whit Monday, Prayer over the Offerings.

this active taking part is the first, indeed it is the necessary, source from which the faithful may be expected to draw the true Christian spirit. Therefore, by proper education it is to be zealously sought after by the shepherds of souls in all their pastoral work.

Moreover, since it cannot be hoped that this will occur unless the pastors themselves are, first, so thoroughly imbued with the spirit and power of the Liturgy as to become past masters in it, there is an even greater need to make the best possible provision for the liturgical education of the clergy. To this end, the Sacred Council has decided on the following measures.

15. Professors who are charged with teaching the subject Sacred Liturgy in seminaries, the houses of studies of religious, and theological faculties, are to receive a thorough training for their task in institutes specially appointed for this purpose.

16. Sacred Liturgy as a subject in seminaries and the houses of studies of religious is to be considered one of the necessary, key subjects; in theological faculties it will rank as a major subject (*disciplina principalis*); it will be taught not only under its theological and historical aspects, but also under its spiritual, pastoral and juridical aspects. Professors of other disciplines, more particularly Dogmatic Theology, Holy Scripture, Spiritual and Pastoral Theology, will take good care, each according to the intrinsic requirements of his particular subject, to explore the riches of the mystery of Christ and of redemptive history in such a way as to make abundantly obvious both their connexion with the Liturgy and the whole unity of the clerical education given.

17. Clerical students in seminaries and religious houses are to receive a liturgical education to the spiritual life. This will comprise suitable guidance to enable them to understand the sacred rites and join in them wholeheartedly; it will also include the actual celebration of the holy mysteries, as well as other devotional exercises steeped in the spirit of the sacred Liturgy. In addition, they

will learn to observe the liturgical laws, so that life in the seminaries and religious institutes may be wholly penetrated by the liturgical spirit.

18. Priests, both secular and religious, already at work in the Lord's vineyard, are to be helped by all opportune means to gain an ever increasing understanding of what they are doing when they celebrate the functions of the Church; they are to be helped to lead a liturgical life and to share this with the faithful entrusted to them.

19. As for the faithful, their liturgical education and active participation - both internal and external, - according to their age, status, mode of life and degree of religious culture, are to be pursued by their pastors with zeal and patience. These latter will know that in this they are performing one of the greatest tasks of the faithful dispenser of God's mysteries. Let them lead their flock in this domain by example as well as by word.

20. Any radio or television broadcasts of church services, especially if they concern the Holy Sacrifice, must be produced with dignity and taste, under the direction and responsibility of some fit person appointed by the bishops.

III. THE REFORM OF THE SACRED LITURGY

21. In order that the Christian people may the more surely gain an abundance of graces in the sacred Liturgy, the Church, their loving Mother, desires to apply herself with due care to a general reform of the Liturgy, for the Liturgy consists of a part that is unchangeable because it is divinely instituted and of parts that can be changed. These latter can, and indeed must, vary with the passage of time, if ever they come to contain things not altogether consonant with the real nature of the Liturgy as such, or things that are no longer appropriate.

In this restoration, it is important to give to texts and rites a form that will express clearly the sacred content they are meant to signify, a form such that the Christian people will be able to grasp this content as easily as possible and share in it in a full, active, congregational celebration.

Wherefore, the Sacred Council has drawn up these general directives.

A. *General Directives*

22. § 1. The supervision and general ordering of the sacred Liturgy are vested solely in the authority of the Church. This authority resides in the Apostolic See and, according to the terms of the law, in the bishop.

§ 2. In virtue of a power granted by law, the supervision and general ordering of liturgical matters within certain fixed limits also belong to the various sorts of competent territorial assemblies of bishops legitimately constituted.

§ 3. Wherefore, no one else at all, not even a priest, may, of his own authority, add to, take from, or modify anything in the Liturgy.

23. In order that sound tradition may be maintained and, at the same time, that the way may be opened to legitimate progress, the revision of the different parts of the Liturgy is always to be prepared by a thorough theological, historical and pastoral investigation. Moreover, the general laws of the structure and spirit of the Liturgy, and the experience deriving from recent liturgical reform and from a large number of grants of indults, are to be taken into consideration. To conclude, innovations should not be made unless when a real and definite advantage will accrue to the Church and when due care has been taken to ensure that the new forms shall, as it were, grow out organically from those already existing.

In addition, steps should be taken to see that, as far as possible, no notable differences in rites arise between neighbouring regions.

24. The importance of Holy Scripture in the celebration of the Liturgy is very great. From it come the passages that are read and expounded in the homily, and the psalms that are sung. Inspired and suggested by it, prayers, collects and liturgical hymns pour forth. From it liturgical actions and signs receive their meaning.

Therefore, in order to provide for the restoration, progress and adaptation of the Liturgy, it is important to spread that keen and loving affection for Holy Scripture that is attested by the venerable tradition of the rites of both East and West.

25. The liturgical books are to be revised as soon as possible. For this work experts must be employed and the bishops of different parts of the world consulted.

B. *Directives drawn from the Nature of the Liturgy as a Hierarchical and Congregational Action*

26. Liturgical services are not private activities but celebrations of the Church, the 'sacrament of unity', that is, a holy people gathered together and drawn up in order under the bishops.[33]

That is why the liturgical services belong to the whole body of the Church, why they manifest it and affect it, and why they also affect its individual members, but in different ways varying with the diversification of their orders, tasks and effective participation.

27. Whenever any rite, of its very nature, implies a congregational celebration with the attendance and active participation of the faithful, let it be emphatically taught that this congregational celebration is to be preferred, as far as possible, to any individual and more or less private celebration.

This is particularly true of the celebration of Mass - without prejudice to the unalterably public and social nature of each and every Mass - and the administration of the sacraments.

28. In liturgical celebrations, each participant, whether minister or simple member of the faithful, in the performance of his office, is to do all that and only that which belongs to him from the nature of things and the rules of liturgy.

---

[33] ST CYPRIAN, *De Catholicae Ecclesiae Unitate*, 7 (CSEL 3, 1, Vienna, 1868, pp. 215- 6); cf. Ep.,66, 8, 3 (Ed.cit., 3, 2, pp. 732-3).

29. Servers, readers, commentators and members of choirs exercise a true liturgical ministry. Therefore, they are to perform their office with all the sincere devotion and discipline that befit so great a ministry and that the people of God has every right to require of them.

They must, therefore, be zealously instructed in the spirit of the Liturgy, each according to his capacity, and taught how to do in a correct and dignified manner what they have to do.

30. To encourage the people to take an active part, their acclamations, answers, singing of psalms, antiphons and hymns, even their actions, for example gestures and attitudes of body, are to be gone into, and a holy silence should be observed at the appropriate times.

31. In the revision of the liturgical books, let care be taken to see that the rubrics provide for the people's part.

32. In the Liturgy, except for the distinction based on liturgical function and Sacred Order, and except for the honours prescribed by the liturgical laws as due to secular authorities, no differences are to be made between private persons or classes of persons either in the ceremonies or in any outward display.

C. Directives deriving from the Educative and Pastoral Character of the Liturgy

33. Though the Liturgy is above all else the worship of the Divine Majesty, it nevertheless contains a great deal of teaching for the faithful.[34] In the Liturgy God speaks to his people, Christ still proclaims the good news. In their turn the people answer God by their hymns and prayer.

The prayers addressed to God by the priest who presides over the assembly in the person of Christ are proffered in the name of the whole holy people and of all those present. The visible signs

[34] Cf. COUNCIL OF TRENT, Sess. XXII, *Doctrine De Ss. Missae Sacrificio*, 8 (DENZ. 946; Ed. cit., 8, p. 961).

employed by the sacred Liturgy for the signifying of invisible divine realities have been chosen by Christ or the Church. It follows, therefore, that it is not only when the words are read that were 'written for our instruction' (*Rom* 15:4), but also when the Church prays, sings or does something, that the faith of the participants is nourished, their minds are stirred up to offer their reasonable service and duty to God, and they receive in more abundant measure his grace.

That being so, the following general directives must be observed in carrying out the reform.

34. The rites should shine with a noble simplicity, be concise and clear, and avoid useless repetitions. They should be intelligible to the faithful and should not, as a rule, require any considerable explanation.

35. In the Liturgy, the intimate union of rite and word should appear clearly, therefore:

(1) In the services a richer, more varied and more appropriate reading of Holy Scripture should be introduced.

(2) The best place for the sermon, since it is a part of the liturgical action, is to be noted in the rubrics, taking into account the structure of the rite. The ministry of preaching is to be performed properly and with great fidelity. Let it draw, in the first place, on the source of Holy Scripture and the Liturgy, and it will be like a proclamation of God's mighty deeds in redemptive history, i.e. in the mystery of Christ ever present and at work in us, especially in liturgical services.

(3) Instruction of a more directly liturgical nature should also be given in every way possible; and, if necessary, during the rites themselves, but only at the more suitable moments, provision should be made for short addresses by the priest or competent minister, in prescribed terms or words similar to those suggested.

(4) The sacred celebration of the Word of God is to be encouraged on the eves of the greater feasts, on certain weekdays in Advent and Lent and on Sundays and feast days, particularly in places where there is no priest. In this case, a deacon or other person appointed by the bishop should conduct the service.

36. § 1. The use of the Latin tongue is to be maintained in the Latin rites, except where some special law obtains.

§ 2. However, in the Mass, the administration of the sacraments and other parts of the Liturgy, the use of the vernacular can not infrequently be very useful to the people. Therefore, it would be well to grant it some considerable place, above all in the readings and addresses to the congregation, in some prayers and chants, along the lines laid down for this in detail in the chapters that follow.

§ 3. Provided these lines are followed, the decision about the use and extent of the vernacular rests with the competent territorial authority of the Church mentioned in Art. 22, § 2. If the case should arise, this authority is to discuss the question with the bishops of neighbouring regions using the same language and its acts must be approved, i.e. confirmed by the Apostolic See.

§ 4. Any translation of the Latin text into the vernacular destined for use in the Liturgy must be approved by the competent territorial authority of the Church, as above.

D. Directives for the Adapting of the Liturgy to the particular genius and traditions of various peoples

37. In matters that do not affect the faith or good of the whole community, the Church has no desire to impose a rigid uniformity, not even in the Liturgy. On the contrary, she cultivates and develops the mental and spiritual graces and gifts of the different nations and peoples. Anything at all in peoples' customs that is not inescapably identified with superstition and error she examines favourably and, if possible, maintains whole and entire. Sometimes, indeed, she

gives it a place in the Liturgy itself, provided it conforms with the principles of the true, genuine liturgical spirit.

38. On condition that the substantial unity of the Roman rite is preserved, room should be found in the revision of the liturgical books for legitimate variations and adaptations to different groups, regions and peoples, especially in the Missions. This necessity should, on occasion, be kept in mind in the ordering of the rites and the drawing up of the rubrics.

39. Within the limits laid down in the typical editions of the liturgical books, it will depend on the competent territorial authority of the Church mentioned in Art. 22, § 2, to determine any adaptations, particularly in the administration of the sacraments and in sacramentals, processions, the liturgical language, church music and the arts; always, of course, according to the basic lines contained in this Constitution.

40. However, in various places and in differing circumstances, a more fargoing and, consequently, more difficult adaptation may be required. Therefore:

(1) The competent territorial authority of the Church mentioned in Art. 22, § 2, is to consider carefully and wisely, what contributions to divine worship it would be right to accept, in this matter, from the traditions and nature of each people. Any adaptations deemed useful or necessary are to be submitted to the Apostolic See for introduction if its consent is obtained.

(2) In order that any adaptation may be effected with all due care and consideration, the Apostolic See will, if advisable, grant the aforesaid territorial authority of the Church a faculty to allow and conduct the necessary preliminary experiments in certain suitable groups over a fixed period.

(3) Seeing that liturgical laws often entail special difficulties where adaptation is concerned, particularly in the Missions, specialists in the matter dealt with should be present when the laws are being framed.

IV. FOSTERING THE LITURGICAL LIFE
IN DIOCESE AND PARISH

41. The bishop is to be reckoned the great high priest of his flock. From him is derived and on him depends, in some sense, the life in Christ of his faithful.

For this reason, all must hold in the greatest respect the liturgical life of the diocese centred on the bishop, especially in the cathedral. Let them be quite certain that the chief manifestation of the Church is to be found in the full, active participation of the whole holy people of God in the same liturgical services, particularly in the same Eucharist - in one prayer at one altar - presided over by the bishop surrounded by his whole body of priests and subordinate ministers.[35]

42. Since the bishop in his Church cannot himself always and everywhere preside over his whole flock, he needs must set up groups of the faithful, and among these the chief are the parishes established on a local basis having each its pastor who takes the bishop's place. These, in some sort, represent the worldwide visible Church.

For this reason, the liturgical life of the parish and its relation to the bishop should be fostered in the theory and practice of clergy and faithful alike. Efforts should be made to encourage a real parish community sense, above all in the common celebration of the Sunday Mass.

V. THE PROMOTING OF
PASTORAL LITURGICAL ACTIVITY

43. The interest shown in the encouragement and restoration of the Liturgy is rightly held to be a sign of God's providential dispositions in favour of our time, as a visiting of his Church by the Holy Spirit. Indeed, it gives a characteristic distinguishing mark to

---

[35] Cf. St Ignatius of Antioch, Ad Magn., 7; Ad Phil, 4; Ad Smyrn., 8.

the Church's life and to the whole religious thought and practice of our time.

To give still greater encouragement to this pastoral liturgical activity in the Church, the Sacred Council decrees:

44. It will be useful if the competent territorial authority of the Church mentioned in Art. 22, § 2, will appoint a Liturgical Commission with the aid of experts in liturgical matters, music, sacred art and the pastoral ministry. Of assistance to this commission would be, if it could be managed, an Institute of Pastoral Liturgy consisting of members of special competence in this domain, among whom might well be, in certain circumstances, lay people. The commission's duty will be, under the guidance of the aforementioned territorial authority of the Church, to direct pastoral liturgical activity in its area, and to further studies and necessary experiments in the case of adaptations to be submitted to the Apostolic See.

45. In the same way, each diocese should have its Liturgical Commission for a furthering of the Liturgy under the bishop's general direction.

Sometimes it might be wise for several dioceses to appoint a single commission for the promotion of the Liturgy on a common basis.

46. In addition to the Liturgical Commission each diocese should appoint, if possible, further Commissions for Church Music and Sacred Art.

These three commissions must work closely together; indeed, quite often it will be best for them to coalesce into one single commission.

CHAPTER II

THE HOLY MYSTERY OF THE EUCHARIST

47. Our Saviour, at the Last Supper on the night on which he was betrayed, instituted the eucharistic Sacrifice of his Body and Blood whereby he might perpetuate the sacrifice of the cross throughout the ages until he should come, and, moreover, entrust to the Church. his beloved Bride, a memorial of his death and resurrection: the sacrament of love, the sign of unity, the bond of charity,[36] the paschal banquet, in which Christ is received, our mind and soul are filled with grace and a pledge is given us of glory to come.[37]

48. Therefore, the Church takes very special care to see that the faithful do not assist at this mystery of faith like strangers or dumb spectators. On the contrary, she wants them to have a good understanding of the mystery through the rites and prayers, and thus to take an intelligent, devout and active part in the sacred action. They should find instruction in the word of God and refreshment at the table of the Lord's Body; they should give thanks to God. Offering the spotless victim not only at the priest's hands, but also, themselves, offering it together with him, they should learn to make the oblation of themselves. Day by day through Christ the Mediator,[38] they should grow into an ever more perfect unity with God and one another, until at last God becomes all things in all of them.

49. Therefore, in order that the sacrifice of the Mass, even in the form of its rites, may obtain its full pastoral effect, the Sacred Council, having in mind those Masses that are celebrated with a congregation, particularly on Sundays and holy days of obligation, makes the following decrees.

---

[36] Cf. St Augustine., *In Ioann. Ev..* Tr, 26, 6, 13; PL 35, 1613.
[37] Roman Breviary, *Corpus Christi*, II Vespers, Antiphon for Magnificat.
[38] Cf. St Cyril of Alexandria, comment. *In Ioann. Ev.*, 11, 11-12; PG 74, 557-64.

50. The Ordinary of the Mass (*Ordo Missae*) is to be revised in a way that will reveal more clearly the real function of each of the parts and the connexions of the various parts with one another. This revision is also to facilitate the devout, active participation of the faithful.

To this end, while the substance of the rites is to be preserved, they themselves should be simplified. Doublets and any additions of little value that have accrued in the course of the centuries are to be omitted. Certain things that have fallen out through the wearing processes of time are to be reinstated after the ancient model of the holy Fathers, according as they may seem advisable or necessary.

51. In order to lay a more richly furnished table of God's Word for the faithful, the larder of the Bible is to be opened up more generously, so that in the space of a fixed number of years, the more important part of Holy Scripture may be read to the people.

52. The homily which, in the course of the liturgical year, uses the sacred text to set forth the mysteries of the faith and the rules of Christian living, is to be strongly recommended, for it is a real part of the liturgy. At Masses celebrated with a congregation on Sundays and holy days of obligation it must not be omitted, unless for a grave reason.

53. 'The common prayer', i.e. 'the prayer of the faithful' ['the bidding prayer'] after the Gospel and the homily, is to be reintroduced, especially on Sundays and holy days of obligation, so that the people may join in and pray for the Holy Church, those in authority over us, those in various troubles and afflictions, as well as for all men and the situation of the whole world.[39]

54. It should be possible to give a fitting place to the vernacular in Masses celebrated with a congregation, especially in the readings and the bidding prayer, and also, depending on local conditions,

---

[39] Cf. *1 Tim* 2:1-2.

in those parts that concern the people, as laid down in Art. 36 of this Constitution.

Provision should be made, however, to see that the faithful can say or sing together in Latin those parts of the Ordinary of the Mass that concern them.

If in any place a wider use of the vernacular in the Mass should seem called for, the measures prescribed in Art.40 of this Constitution are to be followed.

55. The more perfect sharing in the Mass whereby, after the communion of the priest, the faithful receive the Lord's Body from the same sacrifice is greatly recommended.

Communion under both kinds, without prejudice to the dogmatic principles laid down by the Council of Trent,[40] can, if the bishops so rule, be granted to clerics and religious and also to lay people, in cases to be determined by the Apostolic See. Examples would be the giving of communion in an ordination Mass to those just ordained, in a profession Mass to the newly professed, and in a Mass following baptism to the neophytes.

56. The two parts which, in one sense, make up the Mass, that is the Liturgy of the Word and the Eucharistic Liturgy, are so intimately linked that they make up one single act of worship. The Holy Synod, therefore, earnestly exhorts pastors that in their instructions they should zealously teach the faithful to take their part in the whole Mass, especially on Sundays and holy days of obligation.

57. § 1. Concelebration, which is an excellent illustration of the oneness of the priesthood, has remained in use in the Church until the present in both East and West. Therefore, the Council has been pleased to extend the permission to concelebrate to the following cases:

---

[40] Sess. XXI, *Doctrine De Common, sub utraque specie et parvulorum*, 1-3 (DENZ. 930-2; Ed. cit., 8, pp. 698-9).

(1)   (*a*) Maundy Thursday in both the Chrism Mass
and the evening Mass;

(*b*) Masses at Councils, Bishops' Meetings
and Synods;

(*c*) Mass at the Blessing of an Abbot.

(2)   In addition, with the permission of the Ordinary,
whose right it is to judge of the advisability
of concelebration:

(*a*) Conventual Mass and the principal Mass in
churches when the needs of the faithful do not
require that each of the priests present should say
a separate Mass;

(*b*) Masses at any kind of meeting of priests whether
secular or religious.

§ 2. (1) It is the bishop's right to regulate the discipline of
concelebration in his diocese.

(2)   Any priest, however, is always to have the possibility
of celebrating a separate Mass, except that it must
not be at the same time in the same church,
or on Maundy Thursday.

58. A new rite of concelebration is to be composed for insertion in
the Roman Pontifical and Missal.

CHAPTER III

THE OTHER SACRAMENTS
AND THE SACRAMENTALS

59. The end of the sacraments is the sanctification of men, the building of the Body of Christ, and the worship of God, and since they are signs they also have an educative function. They not only suppose faith; they also, by words and objects, nourish, strengthen and express it. This is why they are called 'the sacraments of faith'. To be sure, they confer grace, but their celebration is the best possible means of disposing the faithful for a fruitful reception of this grace, for the fitting worship of God and for the practice of charity.

Hence it follows that it is of the greatest importance that the faithful should be able to understand easily the signs conveyed in the sacraments and that they should be most zealous in their frequentation of those sacraments that were instituted to nourish the Christian life.

60. In addition, Holy Mother Church has instituted sacramentals. These are sacred signs by which, somewhat after the pattern of the sacraments, certain effects - chiefly spiritual ones - are both indicated and, as a result of the Church's advocacy, obtained. The sacramentals have a twofold function: they dispose men for the reception of the chief effect [, that] of the sacraments; they hallow a number of circumstances in the lives of men.

61. As a consequence, those of the faithful who are well disposed find that, in the liturgy of the sacraments and sacramentals, practically every happening of their lives is sanctified by the divine grace that flows from the paschal mystery of the Passion, Death and Resurrection of Christ, the source from which all the sacraments and sacramentals derive their power. Indeed, there is scarcely any right use of material things that cannot be directed to the sanctification of man and the praise of God.

62. However, with the passage of time, certain things have found a place in the rites of both sacraments and sacramentals, that rather obscure to men of our day their real nature and end. In so far as this is so, some adaptations must be made to the needs of our time. The Sacred Council sets out the following rules to govern this revision.

63. As in many cases it may be found extremely useful for the people if the vernacular is adopted in the administration of the sacraments and sacramentals, it is only right that some considerable place should be given to this, as follows:

(*a*) In the administration of the sacraments and sacramentals the vernacular may be used as laid down in Art. 36.

(*b*) In accordance with the new edition of the Roman Ritual, proper Rituals, adapted - in language also - to meet the special needs of each region, are to be prepared as quickly as possible by the competent territorial authority of the Church (see Art. 22, §2 of this Constitution). After inspection by the Apostolic See, they will be used in their respective regions. When these Rituals or proper Smaller Rituals (*Collectiones Rituum*) are being prepared, the instructions - pastoral, rubrical, or of special social importance - that precede the various rites in the Roman Ritual are not to be omitted.

64. An adult catechumenate divided into several stages is to be restored, the introduction of which will depend on the judgement of the local Ordinary. In this way, it should prove possible to sanctify the time of the catechumenate, which is meant to be given over to the fitting instruction of the catechumen, with a succession of sacred rites to be performed each in its right time.

65. In missionary countries, over and above the elements already found in Christian tradition, there should be no difficulty in admitting further initiation ceremonies that may be in use among different peoples, in so far as they can be adapted to the Christian rite, as laid down in Art. 37-40 of this Constitution.

66. Both rites of adult baptism, the simple one and the more solemn that takes account of the restored catechumenate, are to be revised. A proper Mass 'For the Conferring of Baptism' will be inserted in the Roman Missal.

67. The rite of infant baptism is to be revised and made to suit the real state of infants. The roles of both parents and godparents, and their duties also, are to be made more obvious in the rite itself.

68. In the rite of baptism there should be modifications, to be used if the local Ordinary approves, when there is a large number of candidates. A shorter service will also be drawn up to be used, particularly in the Missions, by catechists, and generally, in danger of death, when no priest or deacon may be had, by the faithful.

69. Instead of the rite called *The Supplying of the Ceremonies when Baptism has been Administered without them*, a new and more suitable one is to be devised making it clear that the child, though baptized with the shorter rite, has already been received into the Church.

Another new rite is to be composed for converts to Catholicism who have already been validly baptized. This should indicate that they are being admitted to the communion of the Church.

70. Outside Paschaltide, baptismal water may be blessed in the service of baptism, using the approved shorter form.

71. The rite of confirmation is to be revised in such a way that the intimate connexion of this sacrament with the whole scheme of Christian initiation may become more obvious. Therefore, a renewal of the baptismal promises will fittingly precede the actual reception of the sacrament.

Confirmation may, if convenient, be conferred during Mass. When given outside Mass, a text is to be prepared that can be used as an introduction [to the whole ceremony].

72. The ceremonies and texts of [the sacrament of] penance are to be revised in order that they may express more clearly the nature and effect of the sacrament.

73. 'Extreme Unction', which may also, and indeed preferably, be called 'The Anointing of the Sick', is not a sacrament reserved to those who are at life's last gasp. It follows, therefore, that the time for receiving it has certainly come when a Christian begins to be in danger of death either from sickness or old age.

74. In addition to the separate services of *Anointing of the Sick* and *Viaticum* a single rite is to be drawn up providing for the anointing of the sick person after he has made his confession and before he receives Viaticum.

75. The number of the anointings will be varied according to circumstances, and the prayers in the *Anointing of the Sick* revised so as to suit the various states of the sick people who receive the sacrament.

76. Both the ceremonies and the texts of the ordination services will be revised. The addresses read by the bishop at the beginning of each ordination or consecration may be made in the vernacular.

In the consecration of a bishop, it is allowed that the laying on of hands should be performed by all the bishops present.

77. The marriage service contained in the Roman Ritual is to be revised and enriched; it should indicate more clearly the grace of the sacrament and emphasize the duties of the partners in marriage.

'If any countries have other laudable customs and use other ceremonies in celebrating the sacrament of matrimony, the Holy Synod much desires that these should by all means be retained.'[41]

---

[41] COUNCIL OF TRENT, Sess. XXIV, *De Reformatione*, 1 (Ed. cit., 9, 6, p. 969); cf. Roman Ritual, VIII, 2, 6.

Furthermore, complete liberty is left to the competent territorial authority of the Church (see Art. 22, § 2 of this Constitution) to devise, on the lines of Art. 63, a proper rite in conformity with the customs of the local population, provided the law is observed that a priest is present to ask for and receive the consent of the contracting parties.

78. Marriage is normally to be celebrated during Mass after the Gospel and homily, before the bidding prayer. The prayer over the bride is to be amended to convey that the duty of mutual fidelity obliges bride and bridegroom equally. It may be said in the vernacular.

If, however, the sacrament of matrimony is celebrated without Mass, the Epistle and Gospel from the Wedding Mass are to be read at the beginning of the service and a blessing is always to be given to the bride and bridegroom.

79. The sacramentals will be revised taking into account the overriding principle of an intelligent, active and easy participation on the part of the faithful and considering also the needs of our day. In the revision of Rituals as laid down in Art. 63, new sacramentals may be added, if called for.

'Reserved blessings' are to be very few in number, and even these shall be reserved only to bishops or Ordinaries.

Provision will be made that certain sacramentals, at least in special circumstances and with the Ordinary's approval, may be administered by lay people possessing the requisite qualifications.

80. The rite of the consecration of virgins contained in the Roman Pontifical is to undergo a revision.

In addition, a rite for religious professions and renovations of vows will be drawn up with a view to obtaining more unity, sobriety and dignity. Provided that particular laws are respected, this rite can then be adopted by those who make their profession or renew their vows during Mass.

It will be a praiseworthy thing if religious professions are made during Mass.

81. The funeral rite will give more obvious expression to the paschal character of Christian death and correspond more closely with the conditions and traditions of each country, e.g. in such things as the liturgical colour used.

82. The rite of the burial of infants will be revised and provided with a special Mass.

CHAPTER IV

THE DIVINE OFFICE

83. The High Priest of the New and eternal Covenant, Jesus Christ, when he took human nature, brought with him into this earthly exile that hymn which to all eternity is sung in the courts on high. He draws about him the whole community of men and makes them his companions in singing with him this song of praise.

He continues this priestly task through his Church, which unceasingly praises the Lord and intercedes for the salvation of the whole world, not only by the celebration of the Eucharist, but in other ways too, and chief among these, by the performance of the Divine Office.

84. The Divine Office, as it has come down from ancient Christian tradition, is so composed that the whole course of day and night is consecrated by praise offered to God. Now, when this wonderful song of praise is duly performed by priests and others set aside for this purpose by the Church's ordinance, or by the Christian faithful praying according to the approved form with their priest, then this is truly the voice of the Bride speaking to the Bridegroom, or rather, the prayer of Christ with his Body to the Father.

85. Therefore, all those who offer this service are at that time accomplishing the Church's duty, are at that time sharing in the supreme honour of Christ's Bride, for, as they pay their praises to God, they stand before God's throne in the name of Mother Church.

86. Priests occupied in the sacred pastoral ministry will find an added incentive to the offering of the praise of their Hours with special fervour in their awareness of their need to observe St Paul's precept: 'Pray constantly' (1 *Thess* 5:17). God alone can give efficacy to and produce results from the task at which they labour, he who said: 'Apart from me you can do nothing' (*Jn* 15:5) With this in mind the apostles, when appointing [the first]

deacons, said: 'We will devote ourselves to prayer and to the ministry of the word' (*Acts* 6:4).

87. To achieve a better and more perfect performance of the Divine Office in the present circumstances, whether by priests or by other members of the Church, the Sacred Council, following in this the movement of reform so happily undertaken by the Apostolic See, has been pleased to lay down the following points concerning the Office in the Roman rite.

88. Since the end of the Office is the sanctification of the day, the traditional cycle of the Hours will be restored in such a way that, as far as possible, its true correspondence in time shall once more be given to each Hour. This will be done taking into account the conditions of present-day life as these affect those, above all, who are occupied in apostolic labours.

89. Therefore, in revising the Office, these principles will be followed:

(*a*)   Lauds, the morning prayer, and Vespers, the evening prayer, which the venerable tradition of the universal Church recognizes as the double hinge of the daily Office, are to be considered and celebrated as the chief Hours.

(*b*)   Compline will be drawn up so as to make of it a fitting end to the day.

(*c*)   The Hour called Matins, though retaining in choir its nature as a nocturnal [offering of] praise, will be adapted so that it can be recited at any hour of the day, and will be composed of fewer psalms and longer readings.

(*d*)   Prime will be deleted.

(*e*)   In choir, the Lesser Hours of Terce, Sext and None will be maintained. When the Office is not recited in choir, it is allowed to choose one of the three corresponding most nearly to the time of day.

41

90. Furthermore, since the Divine Office, the Church's public prayer, is the fountain of devotion and food of personal prayer, priests and all others who take part in the Divine Office are begged in the Lord [to see to it] that, when they perform it, their minds should accord with their voices. That they may the better achieve this, they should set about acquiring a rich liturgical and biblical culture, particularly as concerns the psalms.

In the work of revision, the venerable, age-old treasure of the Roman Office should be adapted in such a way that all those to whom it is committed may more easily find in it still more abundant fruit.

91. In order that it may be practically possible to keep to the cycle of Hours set out in Art. 89, the psalms will no longer be distributed over one week but over some longer period.

The work of revising the Psalter, already happily begun, will be concluded as quickly as possible, giving due consideration to [the following points:] Christian Latinity, liturgical use including [the requirements of] singing, the whole tradition of the Latin Church.

92. In the matter of the readings, these are the points to be noted:

(a) The reading of Holy Scripture will be arranged so that the treasures of God's Word may be made readily accessible in yet greater fullness.

(b) The lessons to be taken from the Fathers, Doctors and ecclesiastical writers will be better chosen.

(c) The 'Passions' or lives of the saints will be given in versions that are historically true.

93. The hymns, in so far as it may seem desirable, will be re-established in their original text, with the removal or modification of any mythological elements or things that have little place in Christian piety. Other texts contained in the Church's treasury of hymns may also be adopted in suitable cases.

94. It is better, both for the real sanctification of the day and for the spiritually fruitful recitation of the Hours themselves, if the time

chosen for their performance corresponds closely to the real time of each canonical Hour.

95. Communities with the obligation of Office in choir, must, in addition to the conventual Mass, perform the Divine Office in choir each day, as follows:

(*a*) Orders of canons, monks and nuns, as well as of other regulars bound to choir either by law or by their constitutions, must say the whole Office.

(*b*) Cathedral or collegiate chapters must say those parts of the Office with which they are charged by the common or a particular law.

(*c*) All members of the above communities who are either in Major Orders or solemnly professed - lay brothers and sisters excepted - must recite alone those canonical Hours they do not perform in choir.

96. Clerics who are not bound to choir, if they are in Major Orders, have the obligation of performing the whole Office every day as laid down in Art. 89. This they can do either in common or alone.

97. Occasional substitution for the Divine Office of some liturgical function will be laid down by the rubrics.

In particular cases and for a just cause, Ordinaries can dispense their subjects from the obligation of reciting either the whole Office or a part thereof, or can replace it with something else.

98. The members of any Institute dedicated to the pursuit of perfection who, in accordance with their constitutions, perform certain parts of the Divine Office, engage in the public prayer of the Church.

Similarly, they engage in the public prayer of the Church, if, in accordance with their constitutions, they recite some kind of Little Office, provided this reproduces the pattern of the Divine Office and is duly approved.

99. Since the Divine Office is the voice of the Church, that is, of the whole Mystical Body engaged in the public praise of God, it is suggested that some part at least of the Divine Office might well be recited in common by clerics who are not obliged to choir, and more especially by priests, where these live in the same house or when they meet together.

All those who perform the Office in choir or in common should accomplish the task entrusted to them as perfectly as they can, with real internal devotion and external decorum.

It is better, moreover, that, when possible, the Office in choir and in common should be sung.

100. Pastors should see to it that the chief Hours, Vespers particularly, are celebrated in common in church on Sundays and great feasts. The recitation of the Divine Office by lay folk either with priests or in their own gatherings or, indeed, by themselves each one alone, is commended.

101. § 1. In accordance with the age-old tradition of the Latin rite, Latin is to be maintained by clerics in the Divine Office. However, the Ordinary is given authority to concede the use of a vernacular version compiled in conformity with the rules of Art. 36. He may use this faculty in particular cases in favour of those clerics who find in the use of Latin a grave impediment to the due performance of the Office.

§2. Nuns, and members of Institutes dedicated to the pursuit of perfection whether men not in orders or women, can receive from their competent superior permission to use the vernacular in the Divine Office even when celebrated in choir, provided the version has been approved.

§ 3. Any cleric bound to the Divine Office who celebrates the Divine Office in the vernacular with a group of the faithful or with the persons mentioned in § 2, satisfies his obligation, provided the text of the translation is an approved one.

CHAPTER V

THE LITURGICAL YEAR

102. A devoted Mother Church has thought it only right that she should, on certain appointed days in the course of the year, hold a sacred celebration recalling the saving work of her divine Bridegroom. Each week, on Sunday, the Lord's day, she remembers the Lord's Resurrection, and again, once a year, at Easter, the greatest solemnity of all, she repeats her experience of the Lord's Resurrection and blessed Passion.

Indeed, as the year passes, she unfolds the whole mystery of Christ from his incarnation and birth to his ascension, to the day of Pentecost and to the awaiting of the blessed hope and appearing of the Lord.

The Church recalls in this fashion the mysteries of redemption, the rich treasures of her Lord's virtues and merits, and opens them up to the faithful in such a way that they may, as it were, be made at all times present. The faithful can thus be brought into contact with them and be filled with the grace of salvation.

103. Celebrating this yearly cycle of the mysteries of Christ, Holy Church venerates with an especial love Blessed Mary the Mother of God who is joined by an unbreakable bond with the saving work of her Son. In her the Church admires and exalts the fruit *par excellence* of the Redemption, joyfully contemplating this unsullied image of what she, in her entirety, desires and hopes to be.

104. In the yearly cycle the Church has also inserted commemorative days in honour of the martyrs and other saints. These holy men and women, brought to perfection through God's manifold gifts of grace and having now laid hold on everlasting salvation, sing to God a perfect praise in heaven and intercede for us. In these birthdays of the saints [to eternal life, the Church] proclaims the paschal mystery in the saints who have suffered and been glorified with Christ, sets before the faithful their examples

drawing all men through Christ to the Father, and by their merits obtains the blessings of God's good favour.

105. Finally, throughout the year at various times fixed by tradition, the Church undertakes the further education of the faithful by means of pious exercises for both mind and body, through instruction, prayer and works of penance and mercy.

For these reasons the Sacred Council has been pleased to make the following orders.

106. Following the apostolic tradition that originated on the very day of Christ's resurrection, the Church celebrates the paschal mystery every seventh day, which day is, therefore, rightly called the Lord's day, or Sunday. On this day, Christians must gather together to hear the word of God, to partake of the Eucharist, and, in this way, to call to mind the passion, resurrection and glory of the Lord Jesus, giving thanks to God by whom they 'have been born again to a living hope through the resurrection of Jesus Christ from the dead' (1 *Pet* 1:3). Therefore, Sunday is the first of all feastdays, to be presented to and urged upon the faithful as such, so that it may also become a day of gladness and rest from work. Other celebrations, unless they are really of the very greatest importance, should not take its place, since it is the foundation and nucleus of the whole liturgical year.

107. The liturgical year will be revised. While safeguarding the traditional customs and disciplines connected with sacred seasons, or restoring them to suit the conditions of our day, their proper nature will be retained so that the piety of the faithful may find its due nourishment in the celebration of the mysteries of our redemption in Christ, especially of the paschal mystery. Local adaptations where necessary will be made in accordance with Art. 39 and 40.

108. The attention of the faithful is to be focused, in the first place, on the feasts of the Lord that celebrate throughout the year the mysteries of salvation. This means that the Proper of the Season

must be given its rightful place above the feasts of saints, so that the complete cycle of the mysteries of salvation may be duly observed.

109. The Lenten season bears a twofold character: it creates in the faithful the right dispositions for the celebration of the paschal mystery, chiefly by baptism, on the one hand, calling it to mind and preparing for it, and, on the other hand, by repentance, as it recommends a more zealous listening to the word of God and a more ardent devotion to prayer. This twofold character will be made more plainly apparent in the Liturgy itself and in liturgical instruction. Therefore:

(*a*) The baptismal elements proper to the Lenten liturgy will be used more liberally; certain features from an older tradition will, where advisable, be restored.

(*b*) The same will be done with the penitential elements. As far as instruction is concerned, the faithful will be carefully taught to understand, together with the social consequences of sin, the specific nature of repentance which is a detestation of sin precisely because and in so far as it is an offence against God. In addition, the place of the Church in the whole work of repentance will be taught and prayer for sinners urgently commended.

110. Lenten penance should be not only an inward, individual thing; it should also be an outward, social concern. Penitential practices are to be encouraged and recommended by the authorities mentioned in Art. 22 according to the possibilities of our time and of the various countries concerned, and, also, according to the conditions in which the faithful live.

Let it, however, be a sacred rule that the paschal fast be celebrated everywhere on Good Friday, the day of the Lord's Passion and Death. Where possible, this fast should be continued on Holy Saturday, so that, with hearts and minds free and uplifted, all may come to the joys of the resurrection on Easter Sunday.

111. Traditionally, the saints are honoured in the Church and their genuine relics and images are held in veneration. The feasts of the saints show forth the mighty works of Christ in his servants and provide the faithful with excellent examples they can imitate.

The feasts of the saints should not take the place of the feasts that celebrate the mysteries of salvation. To prevent this from happening, many of these feasts of saints will be left to the celebration of particular Churches, nations or religious families; to the universal Church will be extended only those that commemorate saints who really did have some universal importance.

CHAPTER VI

CHURCH MUSIC

112. In the musical tradition of the universal Church is contained a treasure of inestimable value. It occupies a place higher than that of other art forms chiefly because it is a sacred chant wedded to words and, as such, constitutes a necessary and integral part of solemn liturgy.

Sacred song has, of course, been praised by Holy Scripture,[42] and also by the Fathers and the Roman Pontiffs who, in modern times, following in this the example of St Pius X, have insisted at some length on the role of music in the Lord's service.

So then, the more intimately church music is linked with the liturgical action the holier it will be. This close connexion is achieved in various ways: the music can express prayer more persuasively; it can help in producing unanimity; it can add increased solemnity to the sacred rites. But it is the Church that approves all the forms of true art that possess the necessary qualities; it is the Church that gives them their place in divine worship.

Therefore, the Sacred Council, adhering to the norms and precepts of ecclesiastical discipline and tradition, and keeping in view the end of church music, which is the glory of God and the sanctification of the faithful, makes the following provisions.

113. The work of the Liturgy takes on a nobler form when the divine offices are celebrated solemnly with singing, with the assistance of sacred ministers and with the active participation of the people.

For the language to be used, follow the rules of Art. 36; for Mass, Art. 54; for the sacraments, Art. 63; for the Divine Office, Art. 101.

---

[42] Cf. *Eph* 5:19; *Col* 3:16.

114. The treasury of church music will be maintained and cherished with the greatest care. Choirs will be diligently fostered in their efforts, more particularly in cathedral churches. Bishops and other pastors will take good care to see that in all sung services the whole congregation may be able to take therein the active part that is theirs, as laid down in Art. 28 and 30.

115. Great importance is to be attached to the teaching and practice of music in seminaries, in the novitiates and houses of studies of religious of both sexes, and also in other Catholic institutions and schools. To this end, every care is to be taken to ensure that persons who will be able to assume responsibility for the teaching of church music receive a thorough training.

Any higher institutions for church music that may be founded as opportunity occurs, are recommended.

The musicians themselves, the singers and above all the boys, are to be given a thorough liturgical education.

116. The Church recognizes Gregorian chant as the chant proper to the Roman liturgy. Therefore, other things being equal, it should have the chief place in liturgical functions.

Other kinds of church music, especially polyphony, are by no means excluded from the celebration of divine worship, provided they accord with the spirit of liturgical action, as laid down in Art. 30.

117. The typical edition of the books of Gregorian chant will be completed. Indeed, a more truly critical edition will be prepared of the books already published since St Pius X's restoration.

It will likewise be of advantage if an edition can be prepared containing simpler melodies for use in smaller churches.

118. Popular religious music should be carefully fostered, so that the faithful may be able to raise their voices in their devotions and pious exercises and, indeed, in the liturgical functions themselves, according to the rules and prescriptions of the rubrics.

119. In some countries, particularly in the missionfield, peoples can be found with a musical tradition of their own that plays an important part in their religious and social life. Due esteem should be had for this music and a fitting place found for it both in the moulding of these peoples' religious sense and in the adapting of the pattern of worship to their particular genius, as suggested in Art. 39 and 40.

Therefore, in the musical training of missionaries, great care must be taken to see that, in as far as possible, they may be made capable of furthering the traditional music of these peoples both in the schools and in liturgical worship.

120. The pipe organ is to be held in high honour in the Latin Church as the traditional musical instrument, the sound of which has the power not only to add a wonderful splendour to the Church's ceremonies, but also to lift up men's minds in a remarkable way to God and the things on high.

Other instruments, too, as approved and agreed by the competent territorial authority (see Art. 22, § 2; 37 and 40), can be permitted in divine worship provided they are - or can be made to be - suited to a sacred use, and provided they accord with the dignity of a church building and really contribute to the edification of the faithful.

121. Musicians, filled with the Christian spirit, should feel that they have a vocation to cultivate church music and to enrich its treasure.

They should see that their compositions display the notes of truly sacred music. These compositions should not be of a kind that can be sung only by the larger choirs; they should also be suitable for smaller choirs and encourage an active participation on the part of the whole congregation.

The texts to be set to music should agree with Catholic teaching; indeed, they could best be taken from Holy Scripture and liturgical sources.

Chapter VII

SACRED ART AND CHURCH FURNISHINGS

122. Among the noblest occupations of the human mind we are certainly right in numbering the fine arts and especially religious art and the supreme expression of this latter - sacred art. Of their nature, these are concerned with the infinite divine beauty and with the attempt at expressing it through human endeavour. Their consecration to God and to the furtherance of his praise and glory is manifested by the singleness of their aim, which is to make in their works the greatest possible contribution to the turning of men's thoughts to God.

For this reason, the Church, like a loving mother, has always been a friend of the fine arts. She has trained artists and unfailingly sought out the noble ministry of the arts, chiefly so that the things needed in divine worship should be worthy, comely and beautiful, signs and symbols of the things on high. Furthermore, the Church has, rightly, always looked upon herself as an arbiter of the arts, choosing among artists' works those that are in conformity with the faith, true religion and faithfully preserved traditional laws, and are, moreover, adapted to a sacred use.

The Church has taken particular care to ensure that sacred furnishings should serve as worthy and beautiful instruments to enhance the comeliness of worship, admitting such changes in materials, design or ornament as technical progress has introduced in the course of time.

That being so, the Fathers have been pleased to make the following orders in these matters.

123. The Church has never had its own peculiar artistic style. It has accepted the idiom of each age according to the genius and circumstances of peoples and the requirements of the various rites. In this way, it has, down the centuries, amassed an artistic treasure that must be preserved with every care. The art of our day and of all peoples and countries is to have free exercise in the Church,

provided it can be used in the service of sacred buildings and sacred rites with due reverence and honour. Then it will be able to join its voice in that admirable chorus of glory which the greatest talents have in the past sung to the Catholic faith.

124. Let Ordinaries in their furtherance and encouragement of a truly sacred art take care that their aim is noble beauty rather than mere display. This holds good for sacred vestments and ornaments.

Bishops will take care diligently to keep out of the churches of God and other holy places, works of art opposed to faith and morals and Christian devotion. They will take the same action concerning works that offend true religious feeling either by their corrupt forms or by their lack of art, their mediocrity or their meretricious character.

In the construction of sacred buildings good care will be taken to see that they are designed for the performance of liturgical functions and for the active participation of the faithful.

125. The practice of erecting in churches sacred images for the veneration of the faithful is to be maintained. However, they should not be too numerous and should be arranged in a fitting order, for they must not cause shock or surprise among the Christian people, or give encouragement to aberrant devotion.

126. In judging works of art local Ordinaries will consult their diocesan Commission on Sacred Art and, if the case call for it, other experts, and also the commissions mentioned in Art. 44, 45 and 46.

Ordinaries will keep careful watch to see that sacred furnishings or precious objects, since they are ornaments of God's house, are neither disposed of nor wantonly destroyed.

127. Bishops, either in person or through suitable priests endowed with the necessary skill and a love of art, will take a careful interest in instructing artists in the spirit of sacred art and of the Liturgy.

In addition, it is recommended that schools or academies of sacred art for the education of artists should be established in those places in which it may seem advisable.

All artists who, following their natural bent, intend to serve the glory of God in Holy Church, should always remember that they are dealing with something like a sacred imitation of God the Creator, that their work is with things made for Catholic worship, the edification and devotion of the faithful and their religious instruction.

128. The canons and ecclesiastical statutes concerning the making of external objects that have their place in divine worship, particularly those affecting the due and worthy construction of sacred buildings, the form and fashioning of altars, the nobility, situation and security of the eucharistic tabernacle, the suitability of and the honour due to the baptistry, the appropriate norms for sacred images, decorations and fittings - all these things together with the liturgical books (see Art. 25) will be revised as quickly as possible. Anything unsuited to the revised Liturgy will be corrected or deleted; anything useful will be kept or introduced.

In this domain, especially where the materials and design of sacred furnishings and vestments are concerned, the faculty of making adaptations to local needs and customs is granted to the territorial conferences of bishops, as in Art. 22 of this Constitution.

129. During their philosophical and theological studies, clerical students will receive instruction in the history and evolution of sacred art as well as in the right principles that should underlie the works of sacred art. In this way, they will be enabled to value and preserve the Church's venerable monuments and be ready with informed advice for artists in their work.

130. It would be well if the use of pontifical insignia were reserved to those ecclesiastical persons who enjoy either the episcopal character or some special jurisdiction.

A DECLARATION OF THE SACRED SECOND VATICAN ECUMENICAL COUNCIL ON THE REFORM OF THE CALENDAR

The Sacred Second Vatican Ecumenical Council attaches no little importance to the widespread wish that the feast of Easter should be assigned to a fixed Sunday and the calendar stabilized. Having considered carefully all the possible consequences of the introduction of a new calendar, it makes the following declaration.

1. The Sacred Council raises no objection to seeing the feast of Easter assigned to a fixed Sunday in the Gregorian calendar, provided the interested parties agree, above all those brethren who are separated from the communion of the Apostolic See.

2. Again, the Sacred Council declares that it does not oppose any efforts made in view of introducing a perpetual calendar in secular life.

However, of the various systems now under consideration for establishing and introducing in secular life a perpetual calendar, the Church does not oppose only those that keep and maintain the week of seven days with a Sunday and do not require the intercalation of any days falling outside the week. The point is that the unbroken succession of weeks should remain, unless the very gravest reasons to the contrary can be alleged, and of these the Apostolic See would be judge.

Each and every one of the matters set forth in this Constitution has been approved by the Fathers of the Sacred Council. And We, by the apostolic authority given Us by Christ, together with the Venerable Fathers, approve, decree and ordain its contents in the Holy Spirit, and order that what has been thus decided in council be promulgated to the glory of God.

✠ **PAUL**, *Bishop of the Catholic Church*
St Peter's, Rome, 4 December 1963
The signatures of the Fathers follow.

NOTE ON THE TRANSLATION

The Latin text of the Constitution on the Sacred Liturgy makes a great use of 'jussive subjunctives', i.e. the form literally rendered in English by 'let *x* be done' or '*x* is to be done'. In this translation, these renderings have been adopted very seldom, and, as a rule, the Latin subjunctives are represented by English futures: '*x* will be done'. However, when the Latin, instead of a simple *admittatur* (for example) has *admitti possit* or *admitti valeat,* or an attempt has been made to reproduce this nuance.

The translator's aim has been to provide an accurate translation in something approaching readable English. He has not tried to present a word-for-word crib or an arsenal of weapons for controversialists.

Square brackets [ ] enclose words inserted by the translator. Linking expressions or repetitions necessitated by the breaking up of complex Latin periods are not so marked.